Prime Ministers of Canada

Time of Transition

By Douglas Baldwin and Patricia Baldwin

Weigl

CALGARY
www.weigl.com

Published by Weigl Educational Publishers Limited
6325 10 Street SE
Calgary, Alberta, Canada
T2H 2Z9

Website: www.weigl.com

Library and Archives Canada Cataloguing in Publication

Cline, Beverly Fink, 1951-
      The new nation / Beverly Cline.
(Prime ministers of Canada)
Includes index.
ISBN 1-55388-247-4 (bound).--ISBN 1-55388-246-6 (pbk.)
      1. Prime ministers--Canada--Biography--Juvenile literature.
2. Canada--History--1867-1914--Juvenile literature. I. Title.
II. Series: Prime ministers of Canada (Calgary, Alta.)
FC26.P7C63 2006   j971.009'9   C2006-902474-X

Printed in Canada
1 2 3 4 5 6 7 8 9 0 10 09 08 07 06

Cover: Lester B. Pearson was one of the most internationally respected prime ministers of Canada.

Photo Credits: Glenbow Museum Archives: page 5 (nc-6-11899); **Library and Archives Canada:** pages 4 (C-005327, C-010460, PA-033933, C-001971), 5 (C-00687, PA-128175), 15 (C-000071), 18 (C-006779), 24 (C-024452), 25 (PA-112659), 32 (C-18978), 35 (C-094168); **Saskatchewan Archives:** page 4 (R-D700).

Every reasonable effort has been made to trace ownership and to obtain permission to reprint copyright material. The publishers would be pleased to have any errors or omissions brought to their attention so that they may be corrected in subsequent printings.

We acknowledge the financial support of the Government of Canada through the Book Publishing Industry Development Program (BPIDP) for our publishing activities.

Project Coordinator
Tatiana Tomljanovic

Design
Terry Paulhus

All of the Internet URLs given in the book were valid at the time of publication. However, due to the dynamic nature of the Internet, some addresses may have changed, or sites may have ceased to exist since publication. While the author and publisher regret any inconvenience this may cause readers, no responsibility for any such changes can be accepted by either the author or the publisher.

Contents

Canada's Prime Ministers

Since **Confederation**, there have been 22 Canadian prime ministers. Canada's prime ministers have come from many provinces and cultures. Some of them, such as the first prime minister, John A. Macdonald, were born in other countries. They came to Canada because they, or their parents, decided Canada was the best place to live and raise a family.

Canada's prime ministers are people of many talents and different interests. Some trained as lawyers, while others were journalists, doctors, farmers, writers, teachers, business people, and members of the **civil service**. Some of them fought as soldiers to protect Canada and her allies. All of them had one thing in common. They wanted to make Canada one of the best places in the world to live.

THE NEW NATION (CONFEDERATION TO 1896)

John A. Macdonald
(July 1, 1867–November 5, 1873; October 17, 1878–June 6, 1891)

Alexander Mackenzie
(November 7, 1873–October 8, 1878)

John J. C. Abbott
(June 16, 1891–November 24, 1892)

John S. D. Thompson
(December 5, 1892–December 12, 1894)

Mackenzie Bowell
(December 21, 1894–April 27, 1896)

Charles H. Tupper
(May 1, 1896–July 8, 1896)

TURN OF THE 20ᵀᴴ CENTURY (1896–1920)

Wilfrid Laurier
(July 11, 1896–October 6, 1911)

Robert L. Borden
(October 10, 1911–July 10, 1920)

TIME OF TURMOIL (1920–1948)

 Arthur Meighen
(July 10, 1920–December 29, 1921; June 29, 1926–September 25, 1926)

 Richard B. Bennett
(August 7, 1930–October 23, 1935)

 William Lyon Mackenzie King
(December 29, 1921–June 28, 1926; September 25, 1926–August 7, 1930; October 23, 1935–November 15, 1948)

TIME OF TRANSITION (1948–1968)

TRUDEAU ERA (1968–1984)

 Louis S. Saint Laurent
(November 15, 1948–June 21, 1957)

 John George Diefenbaker
(June 21, 1957–April 22, 1963)

 Lester B. Pearson
(April 22, 1963–April 20, 1968)

 **Pierre Elliott Trudeau**
(April 20, 1968–June 3, 1979; March 3, 1980–June 30, 1984)

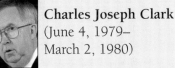 **Charles Joseph Clark**
(June 4, 1979–March 2, 1980)

 John N. Turner
(June 30, 1984–September 17, 1984)

CONTEMPORARY CANADA (1984 TO PRESENT)

 **Martin Brian Mulroney**
(September 17, 1984–June 13, 1993)

 Jean J. Chrétien
(October 25, 1993–December 12, 2003)

Kim Campbell
(June 13, 1993–October 25, 1993)

 Paul E. P. Martin
(December 12, 2003–February 6, 2006)

Stephen J. Harper
(February 6, 2006–)

Louis St. Laurent: Canada's Second French-Canadian Prime Minister

Louis St. Laurent won two consecutive elections and spent many years as the prime minister of Canada.

The decades following World War II were a period of change. The first decade was filled with confidence and **prosperity**. With the end of the war, women returned home from the factories, and men returned home from fighting overseas. Many men and women began families. Canada's "baby boom" began.

The period was also marked by the Cold War and problems with the United States. Canadian prime ministers had to be careful not to favour either the United States or the Soviet Union because favouring one country over the other could potentially alienate one or both countries.

Prime Minister Louis St. Laurent had a relatively easy time winning the elections of 1948 and 1953. National unity was his priority. St. Laurent valued a unified Canada. He was descended from both French and British ancestry, and he was fluently bilingual.

St. Laurent was a patriotic man with a keen intellect. He issued improved social welfare programs, started the St. Lawrence Seaway and the Trans-Canada highway, created the Canada Council, and welcomed Newfoundland into Confederation. He also issued equalizing payments to the provinces, which gave poorer provinces more money.

The economy sagged after St. Laurent left office. Liberal leader Lester Pearson and Conservative leader John Diefenbaker competed to win the country's support.

Before becoming prime minister, St. Laurent was the minister of justice for the Canadian government.

Keeping Canada Together

"Our nation was planned as a political partnership of two great races. It was planned by men of vision, of tolerance, as a partnership in which both partners would retain their essential characteristics, their religion and their culture."
St. Laurent, August 6, 1948

St. Laurent's Early Years

> **"I have always thought that the concept of the father of a family was the best one to be applied to the management of public affairs."**
>
> *St. Laurent*

Louis Stephen St. Laurent was born in the small farming village of Compton, Quebec, on February 1, 1882. His father was French Canadian, and his mother was Irish Canadian. Laurent's family roots in Quebec went back three centuries. He grew up speaking French to his father and English to his mother. He was a teenager before he realized that this was not common practice in every family.

At first, Louis was educated at home. He later attended a religious college to study for the priesthood, but he was more interested in law. In 1905, he graduated with a law degree from Laval University. Louis was an excellent student. Upon graduation, he turned down a **scholarship** to study at Oxford in Great Britain in favour of starting a legal practice. He joined a Quebec law firm and began a 25-year legal career.

St. Laurent's bilingualism was an asset. Soon, he had wealthy clients in Quebec, Ottawa, Great Britain, and the United States. Although his family and many of his friends were strong Liberal supporters, St. Laurent had no interest in being a politician. He married Jeanne Renault in 1908, and the couple had five children.

In 1941, St. Laurent headed the largest law firm in Quebec City. He began to consider retirement.

Laval University was Canada's first university and the first institution in North America to offer higher education in French.

St. Laurent Becomes Prime Minister

In 1941, St. Laurent was sitting at the dinner table with his family when Prime Minister William Lyon Mackenzie King phoned.

"He didn't seem very happy when he came back," St. Laurent's granddaughter later remembered about her granfather. "He said 'Mr. King has called me'—it was during the war—'and I have to go to Ottawa tomorrow.' And my grandmother was quite sad."

Ernest Lapointe, minister of justice and Prime Minister Mackenzie King's Quebec lieutenant, had just died. Mackenzie King needed to replace him with a man of equal stature and ability. His Cabinet had recommended St. Laurent. However, St. Laurent was reluctant to enter politics. He had nothing personal to gain, and he would make less money. St. Laurent accepted on the grounds of patriotic duty, with the agreement that he would retire as soon as the war was over. "I know nothing about politics," St. Laurent told reporters. I'm just 'a good average Canadian.'"

In November 1948, at the age of 66, St. Laurent became prime minister. He encouraged Canada's participation in world events. After World War II, he promoted a more important role for Canada within the United Nations.

His first speech, my mother and her sisters and brothers, everybody went to hear him. It was so terrible, the first speech he made. Then all the family came out and everybody was crying! And they said 'He'll never be elected! He has no talent to speak in public.' Although he was a great lawyer, he was not a politician!"

Louise Mignault,
St. Laurent's granddaughter

Prime Minister Mackenzie King hired St. Laurent as his Quebec lieutenant.

Image is Everything

Although image is a major part of politics today, it was not as important prior to the 1950s. St. Laurent was the first Canadian prime minister to establish a media image.

As a father of five and a grandfather of 12, St. Laurent adored children. On one of his first campaign stops in a small town in Manitoba, he approached a group of children on the railway platform. The children responded enthusiastically to his interest.

In order to enhance his family-friendly image, St. Laurent appeared in casual short-sleeved shirts to deliver speeches. Travelling by train to the United States in 1950, he wore the engineer's cap and overalls, and he drove the locomotive part of the way. Contrary to his casual media image, St. Laurent preferred tailored suits and silk ties. As a former wealthy, corporate lawyer, he was almost always well-dressed.

St. Laurent was portrayed as a gentle grandfather who spoke perfect English. The Liberals used this image, plus St. Laurent's accomplishments in office, to win the 1949 and 1953 elections.

St. Laurent married Jeanne Renault. Their wedding took place on May 19, 1908.

DID YOU KNOW?

During the 1949 election, St. Laurent contracted laryngitis. He could barely talk. "Don't worry," said a Liberal image-maker, "tell him to keep on shaking hands and patting children's heads." St. Laurent took his advice and won by a landslide.

St. Laurent and Canadian Nationalism

As early as 1949, the **federal government** worried about the impact of U.S. **mass media** on Canadian culture. The government was concerned that Canadian culture would stop developing and that U.S. culture would dominate Canada. St. Laurent established a Royal **Commission** on National Development in the Arts, commonly known as the Massey Commission, to investigate Canadian culture, education, and communication.

The Massey Commission released its report in 1951. It noted that there had been a huge growth of music in Canada during the previous 25 years. This growth was due to the new technologies of radio and the phonograph, which allowed people to listen to music without having the musicians present.

Professional orchestras were based in Montreal, Toronto, Vancouver, and Winnipeg. Smaller **municipalities**, however, rarely enjoyed performances by the top Canadian artists. The cost of touring such a large country and U.S. domination of the music industry made it difficult for a young Canadian performer to be successful.

The commission recommended that the government help Canadian musicians, actors, and dancers through federal funding for the arts. In 1957, the St. Laurent government established the Canada Council to promote the arts. It also created the National Library of Canada.

In 1952, the Canadian **Broadcasting** Corporation (CBC) established its own television network to provide Canadian television programs. By 1955, CBC television reached 66 percent of the Canadian population. In 1958, CBC television broadcast for the first time coast-to-coast.

The phonograph was the first device that could record and play sound. It is similar to a record player

> **"I consider that all Canadians have an equal right to benefit from the advantages of belonging to the Canadian nation."**
>
> *St. Laurent*

CANADIAN BORN

St. Laurent appointed the first **governor general** born in Canada, Vincent Massey, to office in 1959. Massey's intense interest in his native land and its people took him to the most remote settlements, from Haida villages in the Queen Charlotte Islands to Arctic Inuit settlements. Of his journey as the first Canadian governor general to fly over the North Pole, Massey wrote, "I found it an experience as humbling as it was fascinating."

New Immigration Policies

In the postwar period, many **immigrants** came to Canada. They felt there were more opportunities in Canada. The new mines and factories needed workers. Over time, immigrants from Italy, Greece, the Ukraine, and other parts of Eastern Europe increased. This changed the face of cities such as Toronto and Montreal. Canada's population now included many more cultures than just British and French.

Under St. Laurent, Canada's immigration policy accepted **refugees**. During the postwar period, **communists** ruled many countries in Eastern Europe. People from countries such as Poland, Hungary, Yugoslavia, and Latvia wanted a new life. To escape communist rule, many came to Canada. They brought their cultural traditions to Canada.

Many of the Hungarian Uprising survivors immigrated to western countries such as Canada.

"I'd been in Canada for a year. My uncle had brought me over to Toronto by paying my fare and letting me stay with him and my aunt. I found later that they had some sort of an assistance program, so they [the government] paid the airplane fare, but that was just for people from Norway and Holland and Germany."

Canadian immigrant

St. Laurent's government provided free transportation to Canada, as well as financial and medical assistance. Although Canada admitted a record number of immigrants by the 1950s, they could not fill the needs of Canada's booming economy.

In response, St. Laurent created the Department of Citizenship and Immigration. Under this law, Canada's economic needs determined how many immigrants were accepted. The government decided to allow more immigrants into Canada. University-educated Europeans and those who knew a skilled trade who could easily integrate into Canadian society were given preference, as well as immigrants from Great Britain, France, and the United States. These people were considered to be best suited to Canada's climate, educational, social, industrial, and labour environments.

The Canadian government allowed the minister of immigration to refuse immigrants on the grounds of nationality, ethnicity, geographical origin, and customs. Visible **minorities** were discouraged.

The sponsorship system was another of St. Laurent's legacies. Canadian residents sponsored thousands of dependent relatives as immigrants to Canada. Toronto received more than 50 percent of all such immigrants.

In 1951, 40 percent of Canadian immigrants were born in Great Britain.

World Issues

St. Laurent wanted Canada to take an active role in international affairs. He thought of Canada as a middle power between the United States and Soviet Union superpowers and the 100 or so less powerful counties.

The tensions of the **Cold War** between the superpowers continued throughout St. Laurent's time in office. After World War II, the Soviet Union sought to expand its control. The United States feared the spread of communism.

Americans and Soviets raced to develop new weapons of mass destruction. In 1952, the United States tested the first hydrogen bomb in the abandoned Bikini area of the Marshall Islands. In 1957, the Soviets successfully launched *Sputnik*, the first artificial satellite in space.

Canada was introduced to the Cold War in 1945, when Igor Gouzenko, a clerk at the Soviet embassy in Ottawa, defected with documents that proved the existence of a Soviet spy ring in Canada. The nuclear arms race left many Canadians fearing that the world was on the verge of nuclear war.

The Cold War tension drew the United States and the Soviet Union into local conflicts in almost every quarter of the globe. One of those conflicts was the Korean War.

After World War II ended in 1945, Korea was divided into two parts. The United States occupied the South, while the Soviet Union dominated the North. In 1947, St. Laurent, as external affairs minister, agreed to have Canadians serve on a United Nations commission to supervise Korean elections.

On June 25, 1950, North Korea invaded its southern neighbour. The United Nations asked its members for help to protect South Korea. St. Laurent agreed to send peacekeeping troops. Twenty-two thousand Canadians fought in that war. Three hundred and nine were killed, 1,202 were injured, and 32 became prisoners of war.

Many Canadian soldiers were wounded or killed during the Korean War.

The Korean War marked a new stage in Canada's development as a nation. Canadian action in Korea was followed by other peacekeeping operations around the world.

Canada had long considered itself safe from overseas attack. In the new era of long-range aircraft and intercontinental missiles, this was no longer true.

In 1949, Canada and the United States joined with 10 Western European countries to form the **North Atlantic Treaty Organisation (NATO)**. Its purpose was to defend Europe and North America from Soviet attack. In 1955, the Soviet Union formed its own alliance with Soviet countries in Eastern Europe. It was called the Warsaw Pact. In the event of an attack by NATO countries, the Warsaw Pact members agreed to come to each other's defence.

The United States feared a Soviet attack across the Arctic. The defence of northern Canada was seen as essential to U.S. security. In 1957, the United States and Canada built a long line of radar warning stations that stretched from Alaska to Baffin Island. They were known as Distant Early Warning (DEW) stations. DEW stations were built to monitor airspace activity. If any of the 50 stations detected missiles or aircraft of unknown origin, it sent a message to North American Aerospace Defense Command (NORAD) headquarters in Colorado.

NORAD united North-American air defence under a U.S. commander-in-chief and a Canadian deputy. It was conceived in the final days of St. Laurent's government and approved by John Diefenbaker's new Conservative government in 1957. NORAD joined Canadian and U.S. fighter planes and missile and radar units under a single command centre. This centre is located deep inside a mountain in Colorado.

World leaders of NATO countries gathered regularly at conferences in cities such as Paris to discuss defence tactics for European and North American countries.

St. Laurent and the United States

The 1950s saw the continuing increase of U.S. economic and cultural influence in Canada. Trade between the two countries flourished. The United States provided about 70 percent of Canada's imports. Canada's exports to the United States represented 59 percent of total exports. By contrast, Great Britain bought only 16 percent. Increasing U.S. demands fuelled a resource boom in Canada. Exports of uranium, aluminum, lead, zinc, and other minerals rose dramatically.

U.S. investment in Canada also grew. Soon, Americans controlled many Canadian manufacturing, oil, and mining companies. Although some Canadians were worried about Canada's growing economic dependence on the United States, the booming economy satisfied most.

St. Laurent tied Canada's economy cautiously closer to the United States. He negotiated with President Harry S. Truman to build the St. Lawrence Seaway. Construction of the St.

Lawrence Seaway was an example of economic co-operation between Canada and the United States. In 1954, each country agreed to pay for and build the sections of the seaway that were in its territory. Costs of common sections on the St. Lawrence River would be shared. The opening of the St. Lawrence Seaway allowed ships to travel from Lake Superior to the Atlantic Ocean.

Until the St. Lawrence Seaway was constructed, the many rapids along the St. Lawrence River prevented travel upstream from Montreal.

"This long sought-after development is about to be realized. In the St. Lawrence Seaway we have another of the accomplishments which friendship and co-operation between Canada and the United States have made possible. I am confident it will be but one of the many monuments that will bear witness to the good relations between our two nations."

St. Laurent's speech on the construction of the St. Lawrence Seaway, August 10, 1954

St. Laurent's Legacy

St. Laurent was presented to Canadians as a kind, gentle prime minister, interested in giving the country good government. However, he lost the 1957 election to the fiery, energetic Conservative leader, John Diefenbaker.

St. Laurent retired from politics in 1958 and returned to his law practice. For someone who once said, "I know nothing of politics and never had anything to do with politicians," St. Laurent successfully led the country through a period of tremendous change and prosperity.

In retirement, St. Laurent was asked to write his memoirs. He refused. "Who'd want to read them?" he said. St. Laurent died of a heart attack in 1973 at the age of 91.

St. Laurent accomplished many things while in office. He started construction of the St. Lawrence Seaway and implemented the Trans-Canada Highway Act 1949. He appointed the first governor general born in Canada, Vincent Massey, provided provincial equalization payments, gave federal money to provinces for approved hospital insurance programs, and began federal grants to universities. He also established the Canada Council, and created the Department of Citizenship and Immigration and the immigration sponsorship program.

In addition to the positive measures St. Laurent implemented within Canada, he also increased the nation's role in international decision-making. St. Laurent brought Canada into NORAD, promoted Canada's membership in NATO, and is responsible for Canadian participation in the Korean War.

CANADA'S LOUIS ST. LAURENT
Father's word is final.

Louis St. Laurent was featured on the cover of the September 12, 1949, edition of *Time* magazine.

John George Diefenbaker: Defender of Minority Rights

Diefenbaker grew up among immigrants and minority groups, and he closely identified with them.

As a young boy, John George Diefenbaker dreamed of becoming prime minister of Canada. His entire adult life was directed toward politics. Despite many election defeats in his early years, Diefenbaker kept trying. He sought to provide equal rights for minority groups and immigrants, who he believed had been excluded from power and influence in Canada.

When Diefenbaker became prime minister in 1957, he continued to champion minority rights. He passed the Bill of Rights to protect Canadians' basic human rights. He relaxed Canada's immigration policies, which made it easier for people to come to Canada. He appointed the first woman federal **cabinet minister**, Ellen Fairclough, and the first Aboriginal **senator**, James Gladstone, a member of the Blood nation. Diefenbaker also championed human rights outside of Canada and helped to prevent South Africa from becoming a member of the **Commonwealth** as long as it continued its policy of **apartheid**.

Diefenbaker worked to improve the standards of living in different regions of Canada. He developed new export markets for prairie wheat in the Soviet Union and China, and he initiated projects to revive the Maritimes. Even after the defeat of his government in 1963, Diefenbaker continued to represent his riding in the **House of Commons**.

Diefenbaker was less successful in improving the economy and in his relations with the United States. He clashed with President John F. Kennedy over refusing to support U.S. hostilities against communist Cuba. The Kennedy and Diefenbaker administrations also disagreed on air defence plans and nuclear weapons.

Diefenbaker died in 1979. At his funeral, Prime Minister Joe Clark described Diefenbaker as "an **indomitable** man, born to a minority group, raised in a minority region, leader of a minority party, who went on to change the very nature of his country and to change it permanently."

Diefenbaker's government gave Aboriginal Peoples the right to vote in federal elections.

Keeping Canada Together

"I haven't spent a lifetime with this party. I chose it because of certain basic principles and those...were the **empire** relationship of the time, the monarchy, and the preservation of an independent Canada."
Diefenbaker, 1967

Early Life

In office, Diefenbaker invited Canadians to contact him personally. He received 300 letters a week.

John George Diefenbaker was born to William and Mary Diefenbaker on September 18, 1895, in Neustadt, Ontario. William, who was of German ancestry, was a schoolteacher. Mary had Scottish origins. John's early life was spent moving from one town to another as his father sought better-paying jobs. John began his schooling in his father's grade one classroom.

In 1903, the Diefenbakers moved to rural Saskatchewan. They lived in a shack that they had built themselves. It was a three-room house with a little garden patch. John bunked with his uncle in a shed, and his brother slept in the kitchen. Three years later, the family took up farming. For three harsh winters, the family survived by working the land. Later, they moved to Saskatoon, where William found work as a clerk.

From the age of 10, Diefenbaker wanted to be prime minister. With his mother's encouragement, John entered the University of Saskatchewan in 1912. His early university marks were average. However, he was a star debater. He earned his master of arts degree in political science and economics in 1916.

Meanwhile, World War I had begun. After graduation, Diefenbaker joined the army and was made a lieutenant. After a few months overseas, Diefenbaker was declared medically unfit for service at the **front**. He returned to Canada.

After returning to Saskatoon, Diefenbaker earned his law degree. In 1919, he opened his first office in a small town 70 kilometres north of Saskatoon. Diefenbaker was a masterful criminal defence lawyer. He won over juries with his stage presence and command of the law. For example, in the **Supreme Court** of British Columbia, he fell on the floor, clutching his throat, to show how a murder had been committed. Diefenbaker represented clients in 20 murder cases. He lost only two. In 1924, he moved his practice to Prince Albert, Saskatchewan.

In 1929, Diefenbaker married Edna Mae Brower, a Saskatoon schoolteacher. In the fall of 1950, Edna was diagnosed with **leukemia**. She died in February 1951. Two years later,

Diefenbaker married Olive Freeman Palmer. She was a senior civil servant in Ontario's Department of Education. Olive had one daughter from a previous marriage that she and Diefenbaker raised together.

> "I know what discrimination is. I know how much easier it would have been for me if my name had been Bannerman, which was my mother's name."
> *Diefenbaker, September 1967*

John Diefenbaker was married twice. His second wife, Olive Freeman Palmer, was a widowed friend from Diefenbaker's youth.

FROM LIBERAL TO CONSERVATIVE

Diefenbaker's passion was politics. His father often told stories about John A. Macdonald and took him to political meetings in the local schoolhouse. Although his father was a Liberal, Diefenbaker became a Conservative. Diefenbaker's memoirs stated that he became a Conservative in the 1911 elections when he realized that "Conservatives stood for one Canada, free from U.S. domination." Diefenbaker was overseas when the **Liberal Party** opposed conscription in World War I. This many have solidified Diefenbaker's change from the Liberal Party to the **Conservative Party**.

Becoming Prime Minister

> "[Diefenbaker] came to the toughest job in the country without having worked for anyone but himself, without ever having hired or fired anyone, and without ever having administered anything more complicated than a walk-up law office."
>
> *Peter C. Newman, writer*

Diefenbaker's political success was a result of his persistence. He ran for **Parliament** in 1925 and 1926. He lost both times. In 1929, he failed to win in the provincial elections. Four years later, Diefenbaker lost the race for mayor of Prince Albert. He finally was elected to Parliament in 1940.

In 1956, Diefenbaker became leader of the Progressive Conservative Party. Prime Minister St. Laurent called an election the next year. While the prime minister ran a quiet campaign, Diefenbaker injected new energy and ideas. He unveiled a new vision for Canada. Diefenbaker promised economic wealth to the Atlantic provinces, the North, and the West. For three months, he led a feverish national campaign.

Canada had never seen a person campaign in the same way as Diefenbaker. He championed the average Canadian. "Everybody is against me but the people," he claimed. According to his Ontario campaign organizer, Diefenbaker "was the best show in town! He loved people, the ordinary people, the average Canadian people. He loved the Prairies. He loved the West. He loved the **underdog**, the farmers. He loved the workers on the railway. He loved the fishermen in Atlantic Canada."

"They criticize me sometimes for being too much concerned with the average Canadian," Diefenbaker said. "I can't help that. I'm just one of them."

In 1958, John Diefenbaker visited northern Quebec, and he received a warm welcome from his supporters.

To the country's surprise, the Progressive Conservative Party won 112 seats. Diefenbaker became the prime minister of a minority government.

The new Diefenbaker government promised support for farmers, loans to buy homes, money for building projects, tax reductions, and increases in old-age pensions and civil service salaries. When the new Liberal leader, Lester Pearson, stated that the Conservative Party should hand power back to the Liberals, Diefenbaker seized the opportunity to call a new election.

"Everywhere I go," Diefenbaker declared in the middle of the 1958 campaign, "I see that uplift in people's eyes that comes from raising their sights to see the vision of Canada in days ahead."

Diefenbaker's campaign swept the country in a wave of enthusiasm. The party's posters told voters to "Follow John." The people responded by giving the Conservatives the largest victory in history.

In 1958, John Diefenbaker attended a rally in Windsor, Ontario, as part of his campaign.

Protecting Minorities

One of Diefenbaker's goals was to create "an unhyphenated nation" in which citizens of many origins and religions would be treated equally. He championed the rights of citizens.

Diefenbaker's call for "unhyphenated" Canadians and for "one nation" angered Quebeckers. They believed that he was unsympathetic to their unique culture. He replied by saying, "I am the first Prime Minister of this country of neither altogether English nor French origin." The idea of an English and French nation, he claimed, would place all Canadians who were not English and French in a position of less importance.

Diefenbaker also championed the rights of Japanese Canadians and **Jehovah's Witnesses**. During World War II, William Lyon Mackenzie King was prime minister, and Diefenbaker was a member of the **opposition**. Diefenbaker did not support the King government's **internment** of Japanese Canadians and the persecution of Jehovah's Witnesses.

When Diefenbaker became prime minister, he granted Aboriginal Peoples the right to vote in

During World War II, when Canada was at war with Japan, Japanese-Canadians were sent by the government to live in internment camps.

federal elections. Prior to 1960, Aboriginal Peoples could not vote in Canadian elections without giving up their **treaty rights** and status as Aboriginal Peoples. Very few were willing to do this.

Diefenbaker improved social programs to provide more aid to the less fortunate. As a supporter of human rights, Diefenbaker was repulsed by apartheid in South Africa. When South Africa became a **republic** in 1960, it had to reapply for membership in the Commonwealth. Great Britain wanted to approve its membership. Diefenbaker, however, agreed with African and Asian Commonwealth countries that South Africa must first abandon apartheid. As a result, South Africa withdrew its application, blaming Diefenbaker. Canada was widely praised internationally for its stance on apartheid.

Diefenbaker also championed equality in the area of immigration. The new government reduced many of the barriers to immigration. For the first time, Canada began to accept larger numbers of Asian and African immigrants.

Diefenbaker promised to protect Canadian citizens' rights. The Bill of Rights guaranteed all citizens that their rights would be respected. The bill was adopted unanimously in August 1960.

The Canadian Bill of Rights recognizes the rights of individuals to life, liberty, personal security, and the enjoyment of property. Prime Minister Pierre Trudeau later incorporated this bill into the Canadian Charter of Rights and Freedoms in 1982.

> **"I know something of what it has meant in the past for some to regard those with names of other than British or French origin as not being that kind of Canadian that those of British or French origin could claim to be."**
>
> *Diefenbaker commenting on the Bill of Rights*

John Diefenbaker was extremely proud of the Bill of Rights and considered drafting it to be a highlight of his political career.

Issues with the United States

> "This government, because of lack of leadership, the breakdown of unity in the Cabinet, and confusion and indecision in dealing with national and international problems, does not have the confidence of the Canadian people."
>
> *Lester Pearson, House of Commons, 1963*

The president of the United States, Dwight Eisenhower, had a friendly relationship with Canadian prime ministers' Louis St. Laurent and John Diefenbaker. As his last official act before leaving office, Eisenhower invited Diefenbaker to the White House for a ceremonial signing of the Columbia River Treaty, an international agreement between Canada and the United States on the development and operation of the upper Columbia River basin. This friendly political relationship died when John Fitzgerald Kennedy became U.S. president. Kennedy was young, brash, wealthy, and sophisticated. His manner grated on Diefenbaker. When Kennedy visited Ottawa in May 1961, tensions intensified.

In 1957, Diefenbaker committed Canada to participate with the United States in the North American Air Defence Agreement (NORAD). The following year, he agreed to create two short-range Bomarc anti-aircraft missile bases in northern Ontario and Quebec. He also agreed to arm the missiles with nuclear warheads.

In February 1959, Diefenbaker cancelled the development and manufacture of the Avro Arrow. The Arrow was a Mach 2 supersonic jet fighter that was being built by a company in Malton, Ontario. Canada would have to rely on U.S.-made Bomarc missiles that only worked when equipped with nuclear warheads. A heated debate within the Conservative Party soon ensued about whether Canada should accept nuclear weapons.

Cuba was the cause of another disagreement between Canada and the United States. In 1962, Soviet nuclear missiles were discovered in Cuba. President Kennedy **blockaded** the island to stop

During the early 1960s, Kennedy and Diefenbaker disagreed about the handling of nuclear weapons.

Soviet vessels from arriving with nuclear warheads. The result was an international crisis. Kennedy called for **solidarity**. Canada had received only a few hours' warning of the U.S. decision to blockade Cuba. Diefenbaker hesitated to put Canadian forces on high alert at Kennedy's request. Eventually, he relented, but it was too late. Many Canadians and Americans perceived Diefenbaker's lack of response as indecisive. Americans were angry, and Canadians were appalled that the government had not co-operated in such a dangerous situation.

In the 1962 election, the Conservatives' majority government was reduced to a minority because of its lack of action during the Cuban Missile Crisis.

DETER, DETECT, AND DEFEND

The motto of NORAD is "Deter, Detect, Defend."
- deter any potential aggressor by ensuring a devastating counterattack
- detect incoming airborne threats with radar and satellite surveillance
- defend North America by coordinating jets and missiles to intercept attackers

A U.S. Navy ship, the *Vesole*, intercepted a missile-carrying Soviet ship, the *Potzunov*, as it left Cuba during the U.S. Naval blockade of Cuba.

Economic Issues and Political Decline

> "He failed in the areas of economic affairs, defense and relations with the United States. He had no capacity to analyze and work through complicated technical problems. This was a failure of intellect, traceable perhaps to his education, his legal experience, and his inability to seek advice."
>
> *Denis Smith, biographer of John Diefenbaker*

Economic problems plagued the Diefenbaker government. In 1961, Canadian unemployment reached 72 percent. Other than economic aid to the western provinces, Diefenbaker seemed unable to decide on any positive policies.

Diefenbaker believed that the policies of the governor of the Bank of Canada, James Coyne, prevented a return to prosperity. Coyne argued that Canada relied too much on exports to the United States. For five months in 1961, Diefenbaker engaged in a public battle with Coyne. Although Coyne resigned, people lost faith in the government, and foreign investors withdrew their money.

Loss of confidence in Canada's economy resulted in a decline in the value of the dollar compared to foreign money. Liberals called the dollar "Diefendollars" or "Diefenbucks."

Diefenbaker carried on as party leader after losing the 1963 election. The Progressive Conservative Party began to splinter. Party President Dalton Camp called a leadership vote. After four rounds of voting, Robert Stanfield was chosen as party leader in 1967.

In March 1958, unemployed auto workers held demonstrations to bring attention to their dissatisfaction with Diefenbaker's government.

Diefenbaker's Legacy

Diefenbaker remained in the House of Commons until his death on August 16, 1979. He won re-election in 1968, 1972, 1974, and 1979.

Diefenbaker's funeral was the most elaborate in Canadian history. For three days, his open casket lay in the parliamentary hall of honour.

From Ottawa, an eight-car funeral train carried the coffin and more than 100 passengers to Prince Albert and Saskatoon. Olive's body was moved from Ottawa to be buried beside her husband, Diefenbaker.

Diefenbaker's love of the "common man" and his support for human rights were his strong points. Until his death, he received letters from Canadians who sought his help.

Diefenbaker has a long list of accomplishments. He helped strengthen the rights of Canadians when he created the Bill of Rights. He changed Canada's immigration policies, making it easier for people to come and live in Canada. He also appointed the first woman to the federal Cabinet, Ellen Fairclough. The Atlantic and Prairie provinces and the fishermen and farmers that formed a large part of the provinces' labour forces did well under Diefenbaker's administration. He provided special money grants to the Atlantic provinces, made wheat acreage payments to farmers, encouraged the Canada Wheat Board to sell wheat to the Soviet Union and China, and developed the Farm Credit Act and Crop Insurance Act.

Diefenbaker also built the South Saskatchewan Dam and promoted the development of the Canadian North.

John Diefenbaker was featured on the cover of the August 5, 1957, issue of *Time*.

Lester Boyles Pearson: Canadian Diplomat

Lester Pearson earned the nickname "Mike" from his squadron commander during World War I.

30

Lester Boyles Pearson had two careers. His first career was as a **diplomat** and foreign affairs expert. He served as Canada's ambassador to the United States from 1945 to 1946. Shortly afterward, Pearson acted as Canada's secretary of state for external affairs for nine years. In 1952, he was president of the United Nations, and in 1957, he won the Nobel Peace Prize for his peacekeeping activities.

Pearson became leader of the Liberal Party in 1958, when St. Laurent retired. In 1963, he became prime minister of Canada. Highlights of his term in office included developing universal medicare, creating the Canada Pension Plan, and the adoption of a new national flag.

Similar to Prime Minister John Diefenbaker, Pearson had a rocky relationship with the United States. The two countries differed on foreign relations, but they became closer on economic matters. The rise of French-Canadian separatism marred Pearson's last few years as prime minister.

> "Under this Flag may our youth find new inspiration for loyalty to Canada; for a patriotism based not on any mean or narrow nationalism, but on the deep and equal pride that all Canadians will feel for every part of this good land."
>
> *Pearson on Canada's new flag, February 15, 1965*

On January 1, 1950, Pearson spoke as Canada's secretary of state for external affairs at the British Commonwealth Foreign Ministers Conference in Ceylon, Sri Lanka.

Keeping Canada Together

"He was a wonderful compromiser, a wonderful person to draw out the compromise. That was his genius. He could bring people in who would be of greatly different views and make them go away smiling."
John English, historian and biographer, 1989

Pearson's Early Life

Lester B. Pearson and his siblings, Marmaduke and Vaughan, attended school in small towns across Ontario. Pearson went on to study at the University of Toronto.

On April 23, 1897, Annie Sarah Bowles gave birth to Lester Bowles Pearson. Pearson's father, Edwin, and his grandfather were both **Methodist** ministers.

Lester was a middle child. He had a younger brother, Vaughan, and an older brother, Marmaduke. All three boys shared their father's enthusiasm for the British Empire and sports. Lester was especially interested in athletics during school, although he also did well academically.

When World War I began, Lester was a student at the University of Toronto. His brothers Marmaduke, or "Duke," and Vaughan enrolled in the war. In April 1915, Lester enlisted and became a private in the Canadian Army Medical Corps. After basic training, he arrived at the front in Greece.

In 1917, Pearson began training in London. Two months later, a bus ran into him during a London blackout. He had constant headaches, trembled, and could not sleep. Pearson was sent home.

After the war, Pearson returned to his studies at the University of Toronto and graduated with a Bachelor of Arts degree in modern history in 1919.

After a year of working odd jobs in places such as a meat-packing plant and a fertilizer company, Pearson was offered a scholarship at Oxford University. He earned a master of arts degree, and joined the history department at the University of Toronto as a teacher. It was here that he met his future wife, Maryon Moody.

At the time, the department of external affairs was looking for intelligent young Canadians to enter Canada's foreign service. Pearson was recruited to work for the foreign service.

Pearson attended numerous important international conferences. In 1935, he was posted to London, England, to report on international affairs. When World War II began, Maryon and Pearson's two children returned to Ottawa. Pearson remained in Great Britain and worked to strengthen British-Canadian ties. He returned to Canada in 1941.

Pearson moved to the Canadian Embassy in Washington in 1942. Three years later, he became Canada's ambassador to the United States. He was now one of Canada's foremost diplomats. In 1946, Prime Minister William Lyon Mackenzie King appointed Pearson as deputy minister of external affairs.

Lester B. Pearson and Maryon Moody married in 1925.

Pearson Becomes Prime Minister

> "There's no question that Mike Pearson loved compromise. My favorite story is about a really complicated constitutional problem that a civil servant had analyzed for him. At the end of this long memo, he had two courses of action that he recommended Pearson take. And Pearson scribbled 'I agree' over both of them! They were completely opposite! He loved compromise."
>
> *Peter Newman, journalist*

In 1948, Lester Pearson won an election to the House of Commons and was appointed minister of external affairs. As minister, he helped lead Canada into the Korean War. The Korean War was a civil war between North Korea and South Korea that involved several other nations, including the Soviet Union and China on the side of the North, and Canada, the United States, and the United Nations on the side of the South.

In 1952, Pearson became president of the United Nations General Assembly. When U.S. General Douglas MacArthur, the commander of the United Nations forces in Korea, spoke about extending the war, Pearson protested. He said that the United Nations must not be the "instrument of any one country."

In 1956, Egypt took control of the Suez Canal from British and French companies. The canal was a vital shipping link between the Middle East and Europe. Great Britain, France, and Israel attacked Egypt. The Soviet Union began to talk of sending volunteers to aid Egypt. Australia backed Great Britain.

Working closely with the United States, Pearson devised a solution. The United Nations would create a peace force called the United Nations Emergency Force that would manage the Suez Canal Crisis and try to prevent conflict. The force consisted of troops from Colombia, Norway, Denmark, Sweden, Finland, and Canada.

In 1957, Lester Pearson received the Nobel Peace Prize for his efforts at resolving the Suez Canal crisis. That same year, Louis St. Laurent lost the election to Diefenbaker's Progressive

Pearson served as a member of Parliament for 15 years before becoming prime minister.

Conservative Party. St. Laurent resigned as Liberal Party leader.

As a recent Nobel Prize winner, Pearson did not have to campaign for the position of party leader. In January 1958, he was elected Liberal Party leader.

Pearson immediately called upon Prime Minister Diefenbaker to resign. Diefenbaker called an election later that year. The Conservatives won 208 seats compared to only 49 for the Liberals. Pearson considered resignation, but was convinced by his friends to stay as party leader.

Diefenbaker narrowly won the next election in 1962, but in 1963, a crisis involving arming Canada with nuclear weapons lost Diefenbaker the next election. The Liberals, under Pearson, were elected with minority governments in 1963 and 1965.

DID YOU KNOW?

Pearson's son, Geoffrey Arthur Holland, followed in his father's diplomatic footsteps. He became ambassador to the Soviet Union in the 1980s and served on various commissions for the United Nations.

Pearson was awarded the Nobel Peace Prize for his role in the resolution of the Suez Canal Crisis. Pearson was given more than $32,000 by the Nobel Foundation.

The Flag Debate

"As the symbol of a new chapter in our national story, our Maple Leaf Flag will become a symbol of that unity... the unity that encourages the equal partnership of two peoples on which this Confederation was founded; the unity also that recognizes the contributions and the cultures of many other races."

Pearson's address on the inauguration of the national flag of Canada, February 15, 1965

One of Pearson's campaign promises was to establish a distinctive Canadian flag within two years of taking office. Shortly after his election in 1963, he asked Canadians to submit their ideas and directed **heraldry** expert John Matheson to work on the flag.

The flag debate divided Canadians between those who wanted to keep the **Red Ensign**, which was Canada's unofficial flag, and nationalists who wanted a new flag.

Diefenbaker was a man of tradition who favoured keeping the Red Ensign as Canada's national flag. When it became clear that the public desired a new flag, Diefenbaker wanted one that honoured Canada's British heritage. He insisted that the **Union Jack** be incorporated into the design. Pearson favoured a design with three maple leaves on a white background that had a blue bar on each side.

When Pearson unveiled the winning design, Diefenbaker was outraged. The parliamentary debate dragged on for 37 days. The government was brought to a standstill. Finally, Pearson used **closure** to put an end to the debate. The majority of the government voted in favour of the new maple leaf flag.

The red maple leaf of the Canadian flag has become a symbol of Canada.

Pearson and U.S. Issues

Pearson moved quickly to repair Canada's relationship with the United States. He had a meeting with President Kennedy. They exchanged baseball stories, and, at the end of the meeting, Pearson agreed to outfit the Bomarc missiles with nuclear arms.

Early in 1965, the United States began an extensive bombing campaign against communist North Vietnam. Pearson called for a halt to air strikes against North Vietnam. The new U.S. president, Lyndon B. Johnson, was not happy with Pearson and shook him by the lapel. From 1966 to 1967, Pearson became more critical of the United States as anti-war sentiment grew.

> "There are some things in politics I don't like, never have liked, and never will like. The hoopla, the circus part. All that sort of thing. It still makes me want to blush."
>
> *Pearson*

By 1967, U.S. exports to Canada totalled nearly $8 billion. The next largest source of Canadian imports, Great Britain, provided only $619 million. Likewise, Canada sent slightly more than $7 billion worth of goods to the United States, and only $1.2 billion to Great Britain. More than 81 percent of foreign investment in Canada was from the United States.

In 1963, Pearson's minister of finance, Walter Gordon, attempted to reduce U.S. investment in Canada. An opinion poll in 1967 showed that more than 60 percent of Canadians wanted the government to change foreign investment policies. U.S. and Canadian businesses did not agree with Gordon's plan. Gordon withdrew the plan.

In January 1965, Pearson and Johnson signed the Canada-United States Automotive Products Agreement. The agreement removed **tariffs** on cars, trucks, buses, tires, and automotive parts. A single North American manufacturing market was created. This allowed Chrysler, Ford, and General Motors to build larger, more efficient manufacturing plants in Canada. The agreement stated that for every car sold in Canada, one had to be built in Canada. Every vehicle built in Canada also had to have at least 60 percent Canadian content in both parts and labour.

Between 1965 and 2002, the number of people employed in the automobile industry rose from 75,000 to 491,000. The number of vehicles made in Canada over the same period jumped from 846,000 to more than 2.6 million.

U.S. companies earned nearly $8 billion from Canadian consumers in 1967.

Pearson and French Canada

> "[It is important] that we make the French-speaking Canadians feel, and they've been in Canada most of them or their forbearers, longer than we have, make them feel like their homeland is not merely Quebec, it's all of Canada!"
>
> *Pearson, 1967*

Quebec's Quiet Revolution was in full gear when Pearson became prime minister. The Quiet Revolution was the period from 1960 to 1966 when Liberal leader Jean Lesage was **premier** of Quebec. Many changes took place under the Lesage government, including overhauling the school system, lowering the legal voting age from 21 to 18, and increasing the provincial budget from $745 million to $2.1 billion. The Quebec government demanded more control over its own affairs. It wanted "special status" within Canada.

The Quiet Revolution escalated on April 21, 1963, when a bomb placed by Quebec separatists killed a janitor working in a Canadian army recruiting office. On May 17, dynamite exploded in mailboxes in Montreal.

In response, Pearson created the Royal Commission on Bilingualism and Biculturalism to recommend ways to strengthen relations between the two "founding peoples" of Canada. The commission toured the country, asking Canadians whether it was important to speak both French and English. Many francophones saw separatism as their only option.

John Lesage was a lawyer and a politician in Quebec. He became premier in 1960.

Pearson's Legacy

Pearson was a distinguished Canadian diplomat. Under Pearson's leadership, the Liberals greatly expanded Canada's social welfare policies, especially universal health insurance and the Canada Pension Plan. Pearson developed the Canada Assistance Plan, created the guaranteed Income Supplement, provided additional funding for universities, and offered students loans. He also developed the the Royal Commission on Bilingualism and Biculturalism.

Pearson kept Canada on the forefront of international affairs by sending peacekeeping forces to the Congo, Cyprus, and the Middle East. He also helped cement the Canadian identity by unveiling the maple leaf Canadian flag.

As prime minister, Pearson never had a majority government. "Everybody likes me," Pearson said. "But they don't vote for me."

In 1967, Pearson announced his plan to resign. Pearson was worried about Canadian unity. He began to work quietly to assure that his successor came from Quebec. He told his closest friends that Pierre Elliott Trudeau was his choice.

In retirement, Pearson lectured on history and political science at Carleton University in Ottawa. He also tried to complete his memoirs. The first volume was published in 1972.

Pearson died of cancer in 1972. As a colleague said, he may have had failings as a prime minister, but he had few failings as a human being.

"[Pearson was] one of the 20th century's most untiring and effective workers in the cause for world peace."
U.S. President Richard Nixon comments upon Pearson's death, 1972

Lester B. Pearson is remembered for his concern for unity within Canada and between nations.

Timeline

1880s	1890s	1900s	1910s
PRIME MINISTERS			
St. Laurent is born on February 1, 1882.	John Diefenbaker is born on September 18, 1895	St. Laurent graduates from Laval University with a law degree in 1905.	Pearson enlists in the Canadian army in 1915. Diefenbaker joins the Canadian army in 1916.
CANADA			
Canada's first kindergarten opens in Toronto in 1883. Calixa Lavallee writes Canada's national anthem in 1880.	James Naismith invents basketball in 1891. Labour Day is celebrated for the first time on September 3, 1894.	Alberta and Saskatchewan become provinces in 1905. L.M. Montgomery publishes *Anne of Green Gables* in 1908.	The first Calgary Stampede takes place on September 2, 1912. The Winnipeg General Strike takes place from May 15 to June 26, 1919.
WORLD			
Thomas Edison invents the light bulb in 1880. Karl Marx, founder of marxism, a communist philosophy, dies in 1883.	Thomas Edison invents the motion picture in 1891.	The Wright brothers fly the first airplane in 1900. Queen Victoria dies in 1901.	World War I takes place between 1914 and 1918.

1920s 1930s 1940s

PRIME MINISTERS

Pearson marries in 1925. Diefenbaker marries his first wife in 1929.

St. Laurent becomes president of the Canadian Bar Association in 1930.

St. Laurent joins William Lyon Mackenzie King's war cabinet in 1942.

St. Laurent becomes prime minister in 1948.

CANADA

Marijuana is made illegal in Canada in 1923.

Banting and Best discover insulin in 1921.

Cairine Wilson becomes Canada's first female senator in 1930.

The Canadian Broadcasting Corporation (CBC) is created in 1936.
Canada declares war on Germany on September 10, 1939.

Canada declares war on Italy on June 10, 1940.

Canada joins the United Nations in 1945.

WORLD

Television is invented in 1929.

Germany attacks Poland on September 1, 1939.

Great Britain declares war on Germany on September 3, 1939.

Japan bombs Pearl Harbor on December 7, 1941.

D-Day takes place on June 6, 1944.

Did You Know?

Louis St. Laurent is the only Canadian prime minister born in the **Eastern Townships**.

The television show *Due South* had a wolf named "Diefenbaker" after the prime minister. The star of the show, Paul Gross, later played Diefenbaker in the mini-series *Prairie Giant*.

A number of nuclear fallout shelters constructed for Canadian government officials during Prime Minister Diefenbaker's time in office were nicknamed "Diefenbunkers."

The National Hockey League gives the Lester B. Pearson Award to the most outstanding player each year.

Pearson had a television installed in his parliamentary office so he could follow baseball games. In April 1969, the Montreal Expos asked Pearson to throw the first pitch at the first Major League Baseball game in Canada.

Major League Baseball's inter-league trophy for games played between the Montreal Expos and the Toronto Blue Jays is called the Pearson Cup.

The Lester B. Pearson Award was first presented in 1971 in honour of the late prime minister.

Test Your Knowledge

Multiple:

Place the following individuals in the order in which they became prime minister.

A) Diefenbaker
B) St. Laurent
C) Mackenzie King
D) Pearson

C), B), A), D)

Multiple:

What political party did Diefenbaker belong to?

A) Liberal
B) Conservative
C) Progressive Conservative

B) Conservative

Multiple:

Which prime minister is most associated with the creation of NATO?

A) Pearson
B) Diefenbaker
C) St. Laurent

C) St. Laurent

Question:

Which countries were considered the superpowers during the Cold War?

The Soviet Union and the United States

Question:

Who appointed Pearson as deputy minister of foreign affairs?

William Lyon Mackenzie King

Question:

Which country's application to the Commonwealth did Canada reject because of apartheid?

South Africa

Question:

What symbol did Diefenbaker want included in the new Canadian flag design?

The Union Jack

Question:

Which prime minister won the Nobel Peace Prize?

Pearson

Question:

What does NATO stand for?

North Atlantic Treaty Organisation

Activity

When Lester Pearson became prime minister in 1963, thousands of different designs for Canada's national flag had been submitted over the years. There were plenty of ideas from which to choose. Pearson created a committee to recommend a design. The committee room walls were plastered with possibilities. As space ran out, members hung their favourite designs from the ceiling.

Many of the designs featured Union Jacks and **fleurs-de-lis**. Others included beavers, caribou, and the North Star. The most popular emblem was the maple leaf.

Pearson unveiled the maple leaf flag at a Canadian Legion meeting in Winnipeg on May 17, 1963. He stated, "I believe that today a flag designed around the maple leaf, will symbolize and be a true reflection of the new Canada." The flag created a storm of protest in Parliament and across the country because not everyone could agree on whether or not to create a new flag design.

DESIGN A FLAG FOR CANADA

Design a flag for Canada. What symbols should be included to represent Canada? What colours should be used, and why? What do they symbolize to you? Should all the major cultural groups be included, and if so, what symbols represent these groups?

Further Research

Books

To find out more about Canadian prime ministers, visit your local library. Most libraries have computers that connect to a database for researching information. If you input a key word, you will be provided with a list of books in the library that contain information on that topic. Non-fiction books are arranged numerically, using their call number. Fiction books are organized alphabetically by the author's last name.

Websites

The World Wide Web is also a good source of information. Reputable websites usually include government sites, educational sites, and online encyclopedias. Visit the following sites to learn more about Canadian prime ministers.

To watch radio and television clips on Lester B. Pearson, visit CBC's archives and click on "Prime Ministers Gallery" and then "Lester B. Pearson: from Peacemaker to Prime Minister."
http://archives.cbc.ca

Check out a transcript of a televised documentary on St. Laurent produced by the Cable Public Affairs Channel.
www.cpac.ca/PMseries/Louis_StLaurent.pdf

Check out this special Confederation website just for kids.
www.collectionscanada.ca/confederation/kids/index-e.html

Find out where the grave sites of Diefenbaker and other prime ministers are on the Historic Sites and Monuments Board of Canada site. Click on "Grave Sites of Canadian Prime Ministers."
www.pc.gc.ca/clmhc-hsmbc

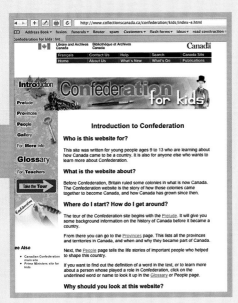

Glossary

apartheid: the policy of economic and political separation of Aboriginal Peoples from the rest of the population in South Africa

blockaded: a closed-off harbor, city, or country by enemy ships or other forces to keep people or supplies from getting through

broadcasting: sending out by radio or television

Cold War: political hostility between the United States and the Soviet Union that began after World War II and lasted until 1990

diplomat: a person who manages relations between countries

Eastern Townships: part of Quebec lying south of the St. Lawrence River Valley and west of Quebec City

empire: Great Britain and its colonies

fleurs-de-lis: designs representing a lily; the unofficial symbol of Quebec and the former royal coat of arms of France

front: the area where active fighting is taking place during a battle

heraldry: the science or art dealing with a coat of arms

immigrants: people who come from another country to live in a new country or region

indomitable: cannot be beaten

internment: forced to stay in a certain place during a war

Jehovah's Witnesses: members of a Christian sect founded in the 1870s

leukemia: a type of cancer

mass media: means of communication that reach a large number of people, such as television

Methodist: a member of any of the Christian churches that grew out of a reform movement within the Church of England

minorities: groups that differ in race, religion, or national origin from the larger part of the population

prosperity: success

Red Ensign: the red Canadian flag until 1965, with the arms of Canada in the centre and Great Britain's flag design in the upper left corner

refugees: people who flee a dangerous country

scholarship: a reward of money to pay for a student's education costs

solidarity: unity between people with common responsibilities and interests

tariffs: taxes on imported goods

underdog: a person that is not expected to win

Union Jack: Great Britain's flag

Political Terms

cabinet minister: an elected member of Parliament chosen by the prime minister to be responsible for a specific area, for example, health or Aboriginal affairs

civil service: an organization of people who work for the administration of the government

closure: a government procedure used to bring a debate to a conclusion by a majority decision of the House

commission: a group of people appointed or elected with authority to accomplish a specific task

Commonwealth: an association of Great Britain and various independent countries

communists: people who follow a political, social, and economic system based on ownership of all property and the means of production and distribution by the community or state

Confederation: the event in 1867 when Canada became its own country

Conservative Party: a party that does not support radical change

federal government: the government of the country, as opposed to provincial or municipal governments

governor general: the representative of the British monarch in Canada

House of Commons: people who have been elected from across Canada to make laws for the whole country

Liberal Party: a party supporting moderate change and reform

municipalities: cities, towns, or other areas with local self-governments

North Atlantic Treaty Organisation (NATO): military alliance of democratic states in Europe and North America

opposition: the elected people whose political party is not the party in power

Parliament: the House of Commons and the Senate

premier: a Canadian province's head of government

republic: a nation in which the citizens elect representatives to manage the government

senator: a representative of the province who reviews laws passed by the House of Commons

Supreme Court: the highest court in Canada

treaty rights: rights guaranteed to Aboriginal Peoples in agreements with the federal government

Index